A PICTURESQUE VOYAGE TO **INDIA;** BY THE WAY OF *CHINA*

A PICTURESQUE VOYAGE TO INDIA; BY THE WAY OF *CHINA*.

BY THOMAS DANIELL

AND

WILLIAM DANIELL

GYAN

Published by

Gyan Publishing House
5, Ansari Road
Daryaganj, New Delhi-110002
Phone: 011-47034999, 9811692060
E-mail: books@gyanbooks.com

Distribution Network
gyanbooks.com
India, USA, Canada, UK, Australia, France

ISBN: 978-93-6433-477-8 (PB)

First Published, 1810

2nd Impression 2023

Printed at: Gyan Press, Delhi.

A PICTURESQUE VOYAGE TO INDIA; BY THE WAY OF CHINA

Author: THOMAS DANIELL AND WILLIAM DANIELL

A

PICTURESQUE VOYAGE

TO

INDIA;

BY THE WAY OF

CHINA.

BY THOMAS DANIELL, R. A.

AND

WILLIAM DANIELL, A.R.A.

LONDON:

PRINTED FOR LONGMAN, HURST, REES, AND ORME, PATERNOSTER-ROW; AND WILLIAM DANIELL, NO. 9, CLEVELAND-STREET, FITZROY-SQUARE.

BY THOMAS DAVISON, WHITEFRIARS.

1810.

INTRODUCTION.

From the earliest era of history the attention of Europe has been drawn to the East; whose fastidious people, vainly disclaiming kindred with other families of mankind, have been implicated in the fate of distant nations, and compelled to endure their unwelcome alliance, or to embrace their suspicious friendship. By a series of political changes, in other quarters of the globe, these countries have been rendered subservient to the feeling or policy of Europe. Curiosity has penetrated the veil of mystery that so long enveloped their civil and religious systems; and their pompous pretensions to antiquity, their venerable laws and institutions, are now exposed to the sacrilegious scrutiny of strangers.

It was an honourable feature in the late century, that the passion for discovery, originally kindled by the thirst for gold, was exalted to higher and nobler aims than commercial speculations. Since this new era of civilization, a liberal spirit of curiosity has prompted undertakings to which avarice lent no incentive, and fortune annexed no reward: associations have been formed, not for piracy, but humanity: science has had her adventurers, and philanthropy her achievements: the shores of Asia have been invaded by a race of students with no rapacity but for lettered relics; by naturalists, whose cruelty extends not to one human inhabitant; by philosophers, ambitious only for the extirpation of error, and the diffusion of truth. It remains for the artist to claim his part in these guiltless spoliations, and to transport to Europe the picturesque beauties of those favoured regions. The contemplation of oriental scenery is interesting to the philosophic eye, from the number of monuments and other venerable objects which still exist in those ever-celebrated countries; and which cast a gleam of traditionary light on the obscurity of departed ages. Happily for curiosity, these vestiges are often elucidated by the manners of the present inhabitants, who with unexampled fidelity have preserved their primitive customs unimpaired by time or conquest; and in their domestic institutions still present the image of a remote and almost obsolete antiquity. There are other associations of sentiment, which in this country must lend to oriental scenery peculiar attractions: a large part of Hindoostan is now annexed to the British empire; and it cannot but afford gratification to our public feelings to become familiar with a country to which we are now attached by the ties of consanguinity and affection. There are, perhaps, few of us who have not been impelled by stronger motives than curiosity to trace the progress of an Indian voyage; and to acquire some local ideas of those distant regions which it has been the fortune of our friends or relatives to explore. To assist the imagination in this erratic flight is the object of the following work: delineation is the only medium by which a faithful description can be given of sensible images: the pencil is narrative to the eye; and however minute in its relations, can scarcely become tedious; its representations are not liable to the omissions of memory, or the misconceptions of fancy; whatever it communicates is a transcript from nature.

GRAVESEND.

Drawn & Engraved by Thos. & Wm. Daniell.

Published by Messrs. Longman, Hurst, Rees & Orme, Paternoster Row [illegible]

GRAVESEND.

THE situation of Gravesend has little to recommend it to the admirers of picturesque beauty. To its tame level shore, however, the Thames presents an animated contrast in the crowded shipping that almost covers its waters. In this promiscuous concourse of vessels, which to a casual observer might suggest the idea of a fair, is exhibited an indescribable and almost inexhaustible variety. Nor are their dimensions more different than their destination: the light shapely sloop gallantly equipt for war, passes before the heavy-laden barge, with difficulty pursuing its homebound course; the elegant yacht with painted awnings, gliding on to music, with no other object than a day of pleasure, is for a time associated with the tough-ribbed Indiaman, so soon to experience the influence of other climates, and pursue its adventurous track on the Atlantic deep. The sprightly group appears on one deck, a care-worn crew the other; here are seen the busy looks of self-importance; and there the tender expression of unutterable regret: the farewell of friends; the lingering glance; the waving hand, still recognized by correspondent signals of affection, all speak to the heart, and extort from it the feeling of sympathetic tenderness.

From the annexed view the town of Gravesend is excluded: the stairs alone being visible. Few who have visited that place would wish to retrace its tumultuous scene of bustle without business, and confusion without variety. If notoriety alone conferred distinction, Gravesend would possess claims to celebrity; few places are so frequently mentioned in English history as the scene of royal embarkation.

PASSING BEECHY-HEAD.

Drawn & Engraved by Thos. & Willm. Daniell.

Published by Messrs. Longman, Hurst, Rees & Orme, Paternoster Row, Jan. 1, 1811.

PASSING BEECHY-HEAD.

AN Indiaman is here represented sailing along the rocky promontory on the south-eastern coast, so well known by the name of Beechy-head. Though still in the vicinity of land, the passenger is already liable to the sufferings and dangers of a voyage, and already experiences the hard privations attendant on maritime life. It is remarked by sir George Staunton, that a private passenger is peculiarly susceptible of happiness, from the ignorance which leaves him wholly dependant on others for his welfare and preservation: "whatever was his situation before he quitted land, it cannot be amended now by the further application of his thoughts to the means of effecting such an alteration; and the train of his labours and solicitudes at least suspended, his mind experiences that calm and rest to which it had probably been hitherto a stranger." The transition from the animated scenes of civilized life, with all its multiplied objects and employments, to the confinement of a ship, is indeed calculated to produce that torpor which should rather be called apathy than rest. Few minds possess sufficient energy to discover in their own reflections a compensation for interrupted habits and pursuits, the suspension of all public and private intelligence, and the absence of all accustomed animation. The interior of a ship presents society under a phasis equally strange and new; it is not a commonwealth on the broad foundation of liberty and equality, but a Chinese system of subordination, with all the minute distinctions of casts, and the watchful jealousy of precedence: it is no community of knowledge; every individual is restricted to his own department, and interferes not with the duties of another: the steward in the cockpit rarely emerges from his submarine sphere to observe the aspect of the heavens or the variations of the wind.

Beechy-head is memorable in history as the scene of that obstinate action between the French fleet and the combined navies of England and Holland in 1692, when the latter were compelled to retreat, and to leave the enemy to insult our shores. Since that epoch our national flag has never been tarnished within the English Channel..

MADEIRA.

Drawn & Engraved by Thos. & Willm. Daniell.

Published by Messrs. Longman, Hurst, Rees & Orme, Paternoster Row

MADEIRA.

AT the first glance the island of Madeira presents the appearance of a rock rising abruptly from the Atlantic ocean. On a nearer approach, the town of Funchal is discovered in a green vale, sheltered by hills and surrounded by foliage, to which its shining white walls form an agreeable contrast. In this view, the Peak castle, standing on an eminence behind the town, the Loo rock, which commands the entrance of the bay, and the solitary religious edifice called the Mountain church, are highly picturesque objects; the houses are embellished with orangeries, and the sides of the adjacent hills are clothed with vineyards and other beautiful plantations.

Tradition attributes the discovery of Madeira to one Roger Macham, an Englishman, who in the reign of Edward the Third is supposed to have been wrecked here with his mistress the beautiful Ann D'Artet. This tale is popular; and the adventures of the unfortunate lovers are painted on the walls of the governor's house. The first settlement formed in this island was undoubtedly by Gonzales Zarco, who in 1419 took possession of it for the Portuguese government.

Madeira is in 32 N. latitude, and 17 W. longitude. It is ten miles in breadth, and fifty-five in length. Its principal produce is wine, but its gardens afford, in addition to the European fruits, the bananas and guavas of tropical regions. The natives are in general of low stature, with dark complexions, and coarse forbidding features. The population amounts to eighty thousand persons. The grey rabbit is the only quadruped existing in a wild state; no venomous animal is here known. The climate is mild and genial, the thermometer being never higher than twenty-five (in the shade) nor lower than sixty-four. According to sir George Staunton, who visited it in October, spring and summer are the only seasons known. "The whole creation seemed alive, myriads of insects were buzzing in the air, swarms of lizards moving along the ground in every direction; scarcely a plant without fruit or flower; every tree in leaf; some of the humble herbs of Europe growing into the form and size of shrubs; nothing appeared languid or declining, unless perhaps man be so considered."

OFF MADEIRA.

Drawn & Engraved by Thos & Willm Daniell.

Published by Messrs Longman, Hurst, Rees & Orme, Paternoster Row [illegible]

OFF MADEIRA.

ON receding from Madeira, the island appears but one mountain, branching in every direction towards the sea. It is common for travellers to make an excursion to the eastern part of the island, in which is discovered the crater of an extinguished volcano. From this circumstance a suspicion has arisen that the island is of volcanic origin; but Dr. Gillan, who had attentively investigated the subject, observed in the chasm of the highest mountains of Madeira hardly any volcanic appearance. "The clouds enveloped frequently their tops, and from them descend all the streams and rivulets of the island. Their antiquity is marked by the deep chasms or gulphs they have formed in their descent between the ridges of the rocks during the long lapse of time they have continued to flow. In the beds of these rivulets are found pebbles of various sizes, and large rounded masses of silex, such as are usually found in the beds of many similar torrents in the Alps. The soil also of the fields and pasturage grounds appears exactly the same as those of the continent, where no volcanic fire has ever been suspected. It is likewise to be observed, that no lava of a glassy nature has been discovered in Madeira, nor any perfect pumice stone." From these observations it should seem that the island is a primary mountain, from which at subsequent periods volcanic matter has been exploded.

To the south of Madeira is discovered a cluster of rocky isles called the Salvages. At the distance of a day's sail appear the Fortunate Isles, or as they are now designated, the Canaries; of these the most celebrated is Teneriffe, distinguished by its gigantic peak, whose elevation equals that of any mountain on the old continent; rising perpendicularly from a ridge of mountains, in whose circuit is experienced almost every variety of temperature. Many volcanic phenomena occur; yet in some the soil is not dissimilar from that of Madeira. The Canaries are subject to Spain; their aboriginal race of inhabitants, the Guanches, are not yet extinct.

CROSSING THE LINE.

Drawn & Engraved by Thos. & Willm. Daniell.

Published by Messrs. Longman, Hurst, Rees & Orme, Paternoster Row, Jany. 1, 1810.

CROSSING THE LINE.

THE day on which a ship crosses the line is commemorated by a humorous nautical ceremony, of which the print is a representation. At noon, the arrival of Neptune is announced; the marine deity is personated by a sailor, bearing in his hand the trident, and seated in a car, which is no other than a water tub, drawn by some of his companions in the character of Tritons. The appearance of Neptune and his retinue is highly grotesque; their oozy locks are composed of long, half-wet swabs, bespattered with oatmeal, and their faces are painted with red ochre. On approaching the captain, Neptune demands the object of his voyage, and receives the customary tribute from those who have not crossed the line, and choose to evade the ceremony of ducking and shaving. Meanwhile the intended victims, including such as have not obtained their freedom from Neptune, are confined between the decks, from whence they are one by one dragged to execution. A large grog-tub, filled with salt water, is placed on one of the gangways, and over it is laid a plank, on which the novice is seated, whilst the barber besmears his face with a composition of tar and grease, and then scrapes it with part of an iron hoop instead of a razor. On the signal being given the plank is withdrawn, when the unfortunate wretch is immersed in water; from which he is not suffered to escape till he is menaced with suffocation. In the plate, Neptune appears with all his retinue, among whom the barber is conspicuous. The ceremony of shaving and ducking is sometimes followed by another, in which the voyager, suspended from the yard-arm, performs an ablution in the sea.

The authority of this custom rests on long established precedent. That its validity is not acknowledged by a legal tribunal, appears from a case which occurred at Bombay in 1802, when an action of assault and battery was brought by a Mr. Maw against certain persons, who had by force compelled him to submit to shaving and ducking. The outrage was clearly proved, and the plaintiff obtained a verdict of 400 rupees.

GALE OFF THE CAPE OF GOOD HOPE.

Drawn & Engraved by Thos. & Willm. Daniell.

Published by Messrs. Longman Hurst Rees & Orme Paternoster Row Feb. 1, 1810.

GALE OFF THE CAPE OF GOOD HOPE.

THE Cape of Good Hope was originally called the *Capo das Tormentos*, the Cape of Storms, an appellation sufficiently descriptive of the rude, inhospitable gales and mountainous billows that impede the navigation in the precinct of its coast. The south-east wind prevails during the winter season, from the end of May to the beginning of September; the north-west reigns through the succeeding months of the year. The steady operation of the south-east wind was observed by Columbus in his first voyage; and it was this circumstance which determined him in returning to Europe to pursue a different track; a practice almost universally imitated by succeeding navigators. When the south-east wind prevails at the Cape, the appearance of the white fleecy cloud, familiarly called the table-cloth, enveloping the summit of Table Mountain, is the presage of an impending storm. "A single glance at the topography of the Cape (says Mr. Barrow), and the adjacent country will be sufficient to explain this phenomenon. The mountainous peninsula is connected with a still more mountainous continent, on which the great ranges run parallel, and at no great distance from the sea-coast. In the heat of the summer season, when the south-east monsoon blows strong at sea, the water taken up by evaporation is borne in the air to the continental mountains; where being condensed, it rests on their summits in the form of a thick cloud. This cloud, and the low dense bank of a fog on the sea, are the precursors of a similar but lighter fleece on the Table Mountain, and of a strong gale of wind in Cape Town from the south-east. These effects may be thus accounted for. the condensed air on the summits of the mountains of the continent, rushes by its superior gravity towards the more rarefied atmosphere over the isthmus; and the vapour it contains is then taken up and held invisible, or in transparent solution. From hence it is carried by the south-east wind towards the Table and its neighbouring mountains, where by condensation from increased temperature and concussion, the air is no longer capable of holding the vapour with which it was loaded, but is obliged to let it go. The atmosphere on the summit of the mountain becomes turbid; the cloud is shortly formed; and hurried by the wind over the verge of the precipice in large fleecy volumes, rolls down the steep sides towards the plain, threatening momentarily to deluge the town; no sooner, however, does it arrive in its descent at the point of temperature equal to that of the atmosphere in which it has floated over the isthmus, than it is once more taken up, and 'vanishes into air;' every other part of the hemisphere shews a clear blue sky, undisturbed by a single vapour.

A MAN OVERBOARD.

Drawn & Engraved by Thos. & Willm. Daniell.

[illegible] Hurst Rees & Orme Paternoster Row [illegible]

A MAN OVERBOARD.

TO check the velocity of a ship in stormy weather suddenly, is often extremely difficult and dangerous; yet it is a necessary operation in effecting the rescue of seamen, who in the performance of their hazardous duties are liable to fall overboard. Messrs. Daniell were witnesses to an accident of this kind, on their voyage, when an unfortunate seaman perished, though every effort was made to save him. A similar event is pathetically described in Falconer's Shipwreck, where four men are swept from the lee yard-arm to the tempestuous deep.

Torn with resistless fury from their hold,
In vain their struggling arms the yard infold;
In vain to grapple flying ropes they try;
The ropes, alas! a solid gripe deny.
Prone on the midnight surge with panting breath
They cry for aid, and long contend with death.
High o'er their heads the rolling billows sweep,
And down they sink in everlasting sleep.
Bereft of power to help, their comrades see
The wretched victims die beneath the lee:
With fruitless sorrow their lost state bemoan,
Perhaps a fatal prelude to their own.

CAPE OF GOOD HOPE.

Drawn & Engraved by Tho.s & Will.m Daniell.

Published by Mess.rs Longman, Hurst, Rees & Orme, Paternoster Row, Feb.y 1, 1809.

CAPE OF GOOD HOPE.

THE Cape of Good Hope is a promontory on the southern coast of Africa, formed of one stupendous mountain, but broken into three distinct masses; each of which has been distinguished by an appropriate name. The Table Mountain, so called because of its flat summit, forming a parallel line with the horizon, appears in this view above Cape Town, and rises to an elevation of 3582 feet. The appearance of this bare, enormous rock, has been aptly compared to the ruined walls of a gigantic fortress. Its north front is flanked on the east by the Devil's hill, which rises 3316 feet; on the west it terminates by the Lion's Head, 2160 feet in height, the summit of which, according to Mr. Barrow, is a solid mass of stone rounded like a work of art, and resembling in some views the dome of St. Paul's church, placed on a high cone-shaped hill. The same author observes, that these three mountains are composed of a multitude of rocky strata, piled on each other in large tabular masses; and that their exact horizontal position indicates not a volcanic, but a Neptunian origin.

The Cape of Good Hope claims supremacy over a large territory in Africa; but the proper Cape district is included in a peninsular tract, eight miles in breadth, and thirty-six in length, from north to south, and united by a low level isthmus to the adjacent continent. Table Bay and False Bay are situated, the one on the north, the other on the south side of the isthmus; and when the former is rendered unsafe to vessels by the north-west gales, the latter affords a safe commodious place of anchorage. Cape Town stands at the head of Table Bay, on an open plain, which leads by a gentle declivity to the foot of the mountain: it is laid out with great neatness and symmetry in strait parallel streets, intersecting each other at right angles, and ornamented in the Dutch taste with rows of oaks and firs, and canals of running water. The town consists of about eleven hundred houses: the fine villas in its environs, with the rich vineyards and delicious gardens interspersed between them, are strikingly contrasted with the solemn, solitary, inhospitable aspect of the neighbouring mountains. The earth is clothed with perpetual verdure: the othonna, an indigenous flower resembling the daisy of England, springs luxuriantly from the trifolium melilotos. The hedges are of myrtle; and the delicate tints of the silver tree are intermingled with the dusky foliage of the oak and stonepine. The vegetable world unfolds its choicest treasures; and the fruits of tropical regions are produced in common with those of Europe. Among the evils incident to this genial climate, may be mentioned the great variety of noxious insects, scorpions, and scolopendras: almost all the snakes are venomous. The horse has been introduced to the Cape. The native ox

ALBATROSS.

Drawn & Engraved by Thos. & Willm. Daniell.

Published by Messrs. Longman, Hurst, Rees & Orme, Paternoster Row, Feb. 1, 1809.

ALBATROSS.

THE albatross, in ornithology the diomedia exulans, has pennated wings, with three toes on each foot, and is about the size of the pelican: it is one of the most curious birds discovered in the tropical regions; it appears to experience great difficulty in ascending from the ground, and is therefore obliged to start from a precipice, or to run for some distance, in order to acquire sufficient impetus to launch into the atmosphere. Its wings, when expanded, extend from nine to twelve feet; with these it cleaves the air, shaping its course with a measured undulating motion. This adventurous bird is capable of long protracted flights; and is often descried by voyagers in far different parts of the globe. Flocks of albatrosses are seen at the Cape; and in the month of June at Kamskatcha, where they are distinguished by the name of the great gulls. The albatross is commonly found in company with the penguin, a much smaller bird, with whom it appears to maintain inviolable friendship., Its natural and inveterate enemy is the petrel, the niocellaria equinoctiales of Linnæus, from whose attacks it can only escape by plunging into the water. The albatross is not known to have any place of incubation in the northern hemisphere; its nests have been discovered in Patagonia and on Falkland's Island, raised one foot from the ground, constructed of clay of a circular form, and indented at the top: the albatross has no sooner hatched her eggs, than the penguin deposits her own in the vacant nest. The food of these birds is supposed to consist of small marine animals. They are sometimes taken with a hook baited with fish, but their flesh is not eatable.

JAVA HEAD.

Drawn & Engraved by Thos. & Willm. Daniell.

Published by Messrs. Longman, Hurst, Rees & Orme, Paternoster Row Feby. 1810.

JAVA HEAD.

JAVA Head is the most westerly point of the island of Java, approximating to the south-east point of the island of Sumatra, from which it is divided by the straits of Sunda. Here the albatross and other tropical birds, distinguished by their long tails and gaudy plumage, again attract the eye; some darting nimbly upon the fish disporting in the glassy deep, whilst others are ensnared by some tempting bait presented to them from a vessel smoothly gliding round the coast. The scenery of Java displays the voluptuous magnificence of the oriental character: on receding from the shore the country assumes a bolder aspect, and is in many parts mountainous; the hills are covered with immense forests impenetrable to man, but tenanted by birds of the most superb plumage. This part of the ocean abounds in sharks: the capture of these voracious animals is always a source of exultation to the sailors, by whom they are held in the utmost abhorrence. To entice them to the ship, a piece of beef in which a hook lies concealed is often let down from the stern; the bait is greedily seized by the rapacious shark, who immediately plunges with it beneath the wave. On detecting the hook he again rises to the surface, and with extreme velocity prepares to make his escape; but the fatal rope continues to be lowered: he is caught in the toils—all his efforts are fruitless; and after a few unavailing struggles he is hauled on board, and extended on the deck; where his destroyers are ready with joyful alacrity to cut up the enormous carcase, reserving the fins and tail for the Chinese market, a rich nutritious soup being, it is said, extracted from those coarse materials.

MALAYE PROAS & CANOES.

Drawn & Engraved by Thos. & Willm. Daniell.

Published by Messrs. Longman, Hurst, Rees & Orme, Paternoster Row, Feb. 1, 1810.

MALAY PROAS AND CANOES.

THE entrance to the straits of Sunda presents a noble sweep of mountains, which rise in a magnificent arch from the bosom of the ocean. The island, which appears to guard the passes of the strait, is called by the French *le grand tocque;* and is more accessible to canoes than European vessels. The construction of the Malay proas cannot but appear strange to a European eye; their canoes are moved by oars equally wide at both ends; a contrivance that enables them to paddle on either side: many of these canoes are so narrow that it is found expedient to keep them steady with bamboo poles, called outriggers. In the structure of these little skiffs, we discover not only the infancy of navigation, but of society; they are obviously adapted to that rude state of mankind in which there is no division of labour, and no co-operation in skill; the efforts of the individual are stimulated by necessity, and have no other object than obtaining the means of subsistence: in such a state of society, an incalculable number of ages might roll away without leaving any vestige of progression or improvement. In the straits of Sunda the attention is forcibly recalled from the contemplation of human art, to the minute but stupendous operations of nature: the sea is here studded with coral islands rising in clusters, which are all comprehended under the name of the Thousand Isles; some of them have a white sandy beach, the resort of turtles; others are skirted with shrubbery to the water edge; they are all flat and low, and the tall trees rising on their level surface have the appearance of masts. The aquatic animals by whose incessant labours they are produced, are classed with the zoophytes; it is scarcely conceivable how such little bodies should supply the materials for so hard a substance. From the soft and leather-like consistence of the tubulated surfaces of the coral fabrics, it would appear, that as the old animals die and their calcareous cells become rigid, succeeding generations continue their operations on the upper and lateral surfaces, each according to the particular form which nature has prescribed. The interior as well as the shore of North Island consists of these substances, for, on examination, at the depth of three feet, were found large blocks of madrepores and various masses of calcareous formation; among other articles, a very large shell of the Chama gigas, supposed to be the largest species of shellfish that exists in the universe. One of the old Dutch navigators observes, that thirty of his people made a very comfortable supper of a single cockle; for the relation of which it may readily be supposed he obtained very little credit. The gigantic Chama which was the Dutchman's cockle, is, however, sufficiently large for the purpose. Near the shores of the island some of these shells are found, of not less weight than four hundred pounds the pair.

ANJERE-POINT STRAITS OF SUNDA.

Drawn & Engraved by Thos. & Willm. Daniell.

Published by Messrs. Longman Hurst Rees & Orme Paternoster Row March 1 1810.

ANJERE POINT.

ANJERE Point is on the Java side, half way up the straits of Sunda; it opens on a range of mountains, some of them rising abruptly in double ridges from the ocean, and others stretching out to the eastern boundary of the horizon. At the distance of some miles from Anjere Point are two small islands called the Cap and Button, which are usually visited by voyagers; unlike the coraline isles, they present steep precipitous banks; and from other circumstances in their configuration are supposed to be of volcanic origin. In the Cap are two caverns open to the sea, constantly frequented by those grey swallows, whose delicate nests form a favourite article of Chinese luxury, and a profitable branch of Javanese commerce. These curious little fabrics are of an oval shape, arranged in regular rows, and composed of fine filaments, cemented together by viscous matter. Nests of a similar structure are discovered in the clefts of the lofty mountains, which rise in the inland part of Java; the swallows that visit these gloomy caverns prey on insects, and are supposed to convert the remnants of their food into materials for their delicate though common habitations. Two months are consumed in the formation of their nests, which are arranged in horizontal rows at different depths, from fifty to five hundred feet. It is usual with the Javanese to attack the settlement three times every year: they descend by ladders constructed of reeds or ropes, according to the depth of the cavern. To direct their march a torch is kindled, supplied by a gum exuding from some neighbouring tree, the light of which is not extinguished by mephitic vapours. Previous to engaging in an enterprize of such imminent risk, it is deemed proper to perform certain religious ceremonies; a buffalo is sacrificed, and invocations addressed to a tutelary goddess, whose priest laying his hand on the adventurers pronounces a solemn benediction: with all these precautions many are left behind to perish in the hazardous achievement. The nests when white and transparent are said to be worth their weight in silver; and thus the occupation that in Europe forms the pastime of the careless school-boy, becomes in Java the most serious and momentous object; and is considered as one of those desperate undertakings which could only be encountered by those hardy sons of penury who willingly barter life for gain.

DUTCH RESIDENCE AT ANJERE-POINT.

Drawn & Engraved by Tho.s & Will.m Daniell.

Published by Mess.rs Longman, Hurst, Rees & Orme, Paternoster Row Mar. 1. 18[illegible]

THE DUTCH RESIDENCE AT ANJERE POINT.

THE Dutch houses at Anjere Point are constructed in the most simple style, and possess little superiority in point of elegance and convenience over the Malay huts; but, like other European edifices, their walls are raised from the ground, and the entrance to them is somewhat more commodious than a bamboo ladder. The situation of this humble village is strikingly beautiful: the partial view of the sea shut in by the neighbouring mountains, the little straits and circles formed at ebb tide between them, though the same spot at high water presents but one smooth waveless expanse; the agreeable intermixture of trees, exhibiting almost every variety of aspect, from the round knotty trunk, to the taper stem and umbellated foliage; all these circumstances conspire to give the place an air of romantic seclusion, and to render it a scene for silence, for meditation, and tranquillity. The natives maintain a profitable intercourse with such vessels as have occasion to stop here to take in provisions and water; the watering place appears in the annexed view. The inhabitants live in ease and security; and the same people who at Batavia consume existence in joyless luxury, at Anjere, under different circumstances, observe those habits of temperance and simplicity which contribute to health, cheerfulness, and longevity.

WATERING PLACE, ANJERE-POINT.

Drawn & Engraved by Thos. & Willm. Daniell.

Published by Messrs. Longman, Hurst, Rees & Orme, Paternoster Row, April 1. 1810.

WATERING PLACE AT ANJERE POINT.

AS a watering place Anjere Point is recommended by its salubrity and convenience. The spring from which the casks are filled is only separated by a narrow ledge of land from the sea; the air is dry and pure, and free from those oppressive fogs so fatally prevalent at North Island and other stations. Provisions of every kind are easily obtained; but it is observed that few esculent fish are caught in the straits of Sunda, a circumstance with great probability attributed to the prodigious numbers of sharks continually prowling near the coast.

The city of Batavia, not far distant from Anjere Point, is placed at the mouth of the river Jucata, on swampy ground, surrounded by stagnant water. This place suggests the melancholy idea of a garden blooming on a grave; the earth teems with delicious fruits, but the air is loaded with pestilential vapours, and vegetation seems to flourish at the expence of human life. Rice is here the most important article of cultivation, the soil is however happily adapted to the production of the spices. The nutmeg-tree, the olive, the cinnamon, the camphor-tree, the pepper-plant, a species of vine whose pungent leaf is the betel, so universally used in the east, are all naturalized to this climate, as is the areca nut-tree, the smallest of the palms, presenting a beautiful miniature of the gigantic cabbage-tree, often the object of admiration in the West Indies. The town of Batavia presents a curious assemblage of inhabitants, collected from different countries, opposed in features and habits, and totally dissonant in language, customs, and manners. A remnant of the Portuguese settlers still exists, blended with the Dutch, and converted to the doctrine of Calvin. A large proportion of the population is composed of Chinese traders, whose thrifty habits and narrow tenements are strongly contrasted with the pomp and luxury of their European neighbours: a considerable number of domestic slaves have been imported from Celebes, and the other eastern islands. The native Javanese not infected with the languor and debility incident to foreigners, and exempted from personal servitude, are among the most numerous, and, perhaps, the happiest members of the community: some of these people have retreated to the mountains, where they preserve their primitive faith and native independence. Whether Pagans or Moslems, they are addicted to the superstitions of their fathers: like the antient Egyptians, they venerate the crocodile; and, like the pacific Gentoos, pay divine honours to the banyan or great Indian fig-tree: little is known respecting the laws and usage established in the interior parts of the island. It is pretended that the emperor of Java has a corps of military females to guard his person; but in all probability this singular institution will be found on investigation to have been as imaginary as the fabulous upas or poison tree of Java, of which Dr. Darwin has given a brilliant description in his Botanic Garden.

MALAYS OF JAVA.

Drawn & Engraved by Thos. & Willm. Daniell.

Published by Messrs. Longman, Hurst, Rees & Orme, Paternoster Row March 1810.

NATIVES OF JAVA.

THE dress of the native Javanese is not dissimilar to that of the Malays, who have settled on their coast. It consists of a close waistcoat without sleeves, fastened at the top with buttons, which are sometimes of gold filigree; over this is thrown the badjoo, or morning gown, close in the front, but confined half way up the arms, with nine buttons to each sleeve. The badjoo proper to young men extends no lower than the waist: it is made of blue or white cotton cloth, chintz, or flowered silk, according to the rank of the wearer. The sayen sorrong resembles a highland plaid; it is of party-coloured cloth, six or eight feet in length, and three or four broad: this garment is either gathered up, and slung over the shoulder like a sash, or folded and tucked about the waist; in full dress it is confined by the criss belt of crimson silk: round the head they bind a fine party-coloured handkerchief, in the manner of a turban, leaving the crown of the head uncovered: when equipt for travelling, they wear the toodong, or umbrella hat. The Javanese, like the Sumatrans, are passionately addicted to gaming; and it seldom happens that one of them is seen without a game-cock under his arm, regularly trained to sport.

A MALAYE VILLAGE.

Drawn & Engraved by Thos. & Willm. Daniell.

Published by Messrs. Longman Hurst Rees & Orme Paternoster Row March 1, 1810.

MALAY VILLAGE.

THE Malay doosoons or villages are frequently situated on the borders of a lake, and generally command an eminence difficult of access. Their houses are raised from the ground on posts or standards, in the manner of the granaries in England; the frames are of wood; the flooring consists of layers of bamboo, over which is a lath of bamboo split thin, and tied down with the filaments of the rattan. This elastic floor is covered with mats of various kinds. The sides of the house are closed in with paloopo, which is the bamboo half split, opened, and rendered flat, by notching the circular joints within side and laying it to dry in the sun, pressed down with weights. The houses are commonly covered with the altass, a species of palm-leaf: the larger houses have three pitches in the roof, the middle one, under which the door is placed, being much lower than the other two: in smaller houses there are but two pitches, and the entrance is in the smaller, which covers a kind of hall or cooking room. The ascent to these dwellings is by a light scaling ladder of notched bamboo, which is seldom fastened to the timbers, and is sometimes taken in at night, to guard against the sudden incursions of ferocious animals. The furniture is simple as the edifice; the bed is no other than a fine mat, with pillows embellished with some shewy material resembling foil; a canopy composed of party coloured cloth is suspended over the head: neither chairs nor tables are necessary articles to the Javanese, who sit on the floor reclining on the left side, supported on the left hand. With the use of knives or spoons they are wholly unacquainted: they use salvers called the doolong, which move on feet; on these are placed the cross waiters, and in them are the cups containing their curry and rice, which, at their meals, is always taken up between the right thumb and fingers. The houses have not the convenience of chimneys; the fire-places are formed of loose bricks or stones, arranged on the landing place before the door.

MALAYE PROAS.

Drawn & Engraved by Thos. & Willm. Daniell.

Published by Messrs. Longman, Hurst, Rees & Orme, Paternoster Row March [illegible]

MALAY PROAS.

THE distant land appearing in this view is the coast of Sumatra, whose deep luxuriant verdure is peculiarly grateful to an European eye; the birds passing like a cloud over the horizon, are a flight of vivacious parroquets, who are often observed pursuing their social migrations from one island to another. In the foreground are two Malay proas, one of which is under sail, the other lying at anchor, and at some distance an Indiaman waiting for refreshments. If the European is struck with the peculiar exterior of the proa, he is equally so by the strange aspect of its crew; he beholds a group of little men, whose lips, disfigured by the unseemly practice of chewing betel, when unclosed, discover teeth as dingy as their complexions; he is addressed in a language wholly new to his ear, but which is rendered perfectly intelligible to his apprehension, by the looks and gestures of the speakers, all eagerly inviting him to purchase their various commodities: one offers parrots and monkeys, another recommends his moosedeer; a third exhibits cages filled with those pretty birds called the ava de vats; every one has a profusion of fruits and vegetables, including cocoa nuts, plantains, yams, tamarinds, and all the luxurious products of a tropical climate. This busy scene of traffic is not calculated to harmonize with the picturesque beauty which prevails in the straits of Sunda, and the eye of taste is unwillingly drawn from the contemplation of nature, to the sordid necessities and turbulent passions of mankind.

MALAYS OF JAVA.

Drawn & Engraved by Thos. & Willm. Daniell.

Published by Messrs. Longman, Hurst, Rees & Orme, Paternoster Row, April 1, 1810.

MALAYS OF JAVA.

THE Malays of Sumatra have nothing to distinguish them from those of Java, in their dress or deportment: the same expression of craft and ferocity is observable in their countenance; they are equally prone to idleness and mischief, to sloth and sensuality, yet are capable of being roused by the hopes of profit to occasional efforts of industry and activity: for their intervals of leisure, they have neither useful nor agreeable occupations, and have no resource but in gaming, to escape from the oppressive melancholy incident to a state of indolent vacuity. The group of loungers in the annexed plate are in this predicament. The neat palisade of bamboos, with a roof of thatch over the entrance, leads to the residence of the Dutch serjeant. In the distance are the two small but celebrated islands of the Cap and Button.

COCOA NUT & BETEL TREES.

Drawn & Engraved by Thos. & Willm. Daniell.

Published by Messrs. Longman, Hurst, Rees & Orme, Paternoster Row April 1.1810.

VIEW WITH COCOA NUT AND BETEL TREES.

THIS view is taken from a delightful spot in the island of Java, which is characterized by its exquisitely soft romantic beauty. The distant land is Sumatra; in the foreground is a cocoa tree, under which is a group of natives, engaged in their favorite amusement of cock-fighting: on the right is a plantation of arecas, the smallest and most elegant of the palm tribe. The areca nut is constantly used in mastication with the betel leaf, which is produced by a creeping plant, of a totally different species: the cocoa delights in a sandy soil, and groves of them are frequently seen extending along the sea shore; it is the patriarchal tree, the object of strong traditionary affection, and the favorite scene of relaxation and enjoyment; to the simple natives it is a constant benefactor; it is employed in the construction of their huts, and the manufacture of their clothing; it supplies nutritious food, and grateful beverage; includes the gratification of wants and luxuries, and is rendered subservient to convenience and ornament. A lively description of the cocoa tree and its multifarious uses is given by a Mahometan traveller, who visited China in the ninth century. 'The people of Oman (says this enterprizing adventurer) go to the cocoa islands, and having felled the tree, with the bark spin a yarn, with which they sew the planks together and so build a ship; of the same wood they cut and round away a mast; of the leaves they weave the sails; and the bark they convert into cordage; having thus completed their vessel, they load her with cocoa nuts, which they carry back to sell at Oman.'

CHINESE TRADING & FISHING VESSELS.

Drawn & Engraved by Thos. & Willm. Daniell.

Published by Messrs. Longman, Hurst, Rees & Orme, Paternoster Row, May 1, 1810.

CHINESE TRADING AND FISHING VESSELS.

THE Chinese vessels, though presenting greater variety in size and structure than the Malay proas, are almost equally inferior to the marine architecture of Europe. The frame, or, more properly speaking, the hull, of these boats, consists of five planks corresponding at each end, the edges being joined together by wooden pins and stitched with threads of the bamboo. Some of the vessels are simply constructed of wicker work, but these like the former are rendered water tight by being completely covered with a cement composed of lime, sea shells, and water; the sails are uniformly of matting, prepared with much ingenuity from the bamboo. The junks though more commodious than the common boats, are not managed with the same facility; they are sometimes launched into the Chinese seas at a considerable distance from the coast, and often meet with destruction, in their perilous conflict with gales which do not endanger the safety of an East Indiaman. The fishing boats, which are good sailors, hover round European vessels and pick up the dead animals which have been consigned to the waves; a striking example of the wretched penury that prevails among the lower classes, and of the difficulty which, with all their activity, they experience in procuring subsistence. The high point of land presented in this view is in 21° 55′ N. lat. and 114° 30′ E. lon. and is known to mariners by the appellation of the Asses Ears. These two gigantic pillars of granite are descried at a considerable distance, towering above the clouds that float in the horizon.

MACAO, CHINA.

Drawn & Engraved by Thos. & Wm. Daniell.

Published by Messrs. Longman, Hurst, Rees & Orme, Paternoster Row June 1 18[illegible]

MACAO.

THE European settlement of Macao is included in a small territory towards the southern extremity of a small island of that name, scarcely eight miles in circumference. It was during the short-lived era of their national glory that the Portuguese obtained possession of this spot, by a grant from the court of China; and in the time of Camoens, who passed here five years of his unfortunate life, Macao engrossed the trade of Japan, and carried on an extensive and lucrative intercourse with the Mogul empire. But these golden advantages have long since been lost, and at present it is only remarkable as a convenient port and a handsome Portuguese town, with a considerable majority of Chinese inhabitants. It is built in the European style, with the singularity of having the laminæ of oyster shells instead of panes of glass in the windows: the same materials have been employed in raising the partition wall, which marks the boundary of the settlement, and is not often passed with impunity, so jealous are the Chinese of the intrusion of foreigners. The residence of the English supercargoes, who spend at this place the long interval of leisure, from March to October, is advantageous to the lazy citizens, who, proud of their bag wigs and swords, abandon to the thrifty Chinese all the useful arts of life. They draw almost all the articles of subsistence from Canton, and in return smuggle opium among the Chinese, whose fondness for this pernicious drug eludes the vigilance and baffles the authority of government. Macao is a place of great natural strength, but its fortifications are unoccupied and untenable; every thing indicates its diminished population and departed prosperity; there are yet thirteen churches for a laity of five thousand people, and for the command of three hundred privates, there exists a considerable military establishment. A situation so confined offers little variety to its inhabitants; but the dulness of the scene is relieved by the fine maritime view, and by the various vessels hovering near the coast. It is from this port that our Indiamen procure pilots for Whampoa. The large three-masted vessel in this plate is a trading junk.

CHINESE HUSBANDMAN.

Drawn & Engraved by Thos. & Willm. Daniell.

Published by Messrs. Longman Hurst Rees & Orme, Paternoster Row June 1 1810.

CHINESE HUSBANDMAN.

THE Chinese farmer, when he conceives it necessary, provides himself with a dress which perfectly secures him from the inconveniences of the weather; this useful suit consists of a cloak and waistcoat, composed of the leaves of the cajam tree, which, like the plumage of aquatic birds, have the curious property of repelling water. The head is protected by an umbrella hat, similar in shape to those in use with the Sumatrans, which shelters the wearer both from the sun and the rain. The hoe in the hand of this man is an implement of most comprehensive use in Chinese agriculture. Sometimes a plough drawn by a buffalo is employed in turning up the ground, but it is a machine of very imperfect construction, and scarcely penetrates four inches below the earth. The Chinese have the practice of steeping the seeds of plants in some liquid manure to accelerate the process of germination; in planting which they are acquainted with the different methods of drilling, dibbling, and broad-casting, but prefer the former, which affords the advantage of superior neatness. They distribute both wheat and cotton in horizontal rows, and are particularly careful to keep them clear from weeds. Danes Island, whence this view is taken, is an islet of small extent, not far from Whampoa, chiefly remarkable for being the rendezvous of European gentlemen who have concerns of honour to discuss: a circumstance so well understood, that at Canton the laconic style of a challenge is, "Danes Island, sir!"

HOTUN, ON THE CANTON RIVER.

Drawn & Engraved by Tho.s & Will.m Daniell.

Published by Mess.rs Longman, Hurst, Rees & Orme, Paternoster Row June 1. 1810

HOTUN ON THE CANTON RIVER.

THE scenery near Hotun presents a specimen of the general aspect of the country on the Tigris, or Canton river. The bordering hills crowned with lofty trees; the gentle acclivities, whose lively verdure is insensibly lost in the deeper foliage of the woods; the solitary pagoda, encircled by trees; the rice fields stretching to the water's edge, and every where intersected by fertilizing streams; these are the general features of the country, and they are such as perpetually delight the eye by their variety, luxuriance, and amenity. Rice is the staff of life in China; it is liable to many accidents from drought and inundation, and is perpetually subject to the depredations of birds and locusts. A total failure in the crops is no rare occurrence, and to this cause, in general, may the frequency of famine be attributed. The pagoda is an object familiar to Chinese landscapes; it does not appear that these religious-looking edifices are consecrated to public or private worship, and they are often introduced for no other purpose than to embellish a fine prospect: it is however probable that these buildings had once a religious destination, but that the associations of thought and feeling connected with their origin have ceased to exist.

CHINESE VESSELS.

Drawn & Engraved by Thos. & Willm. Daniell.

Published by Messrs. Longman, Hurst, Rees & Orme, Paternoster Row, June 1 1810.

CHINESE VESSELS.

THE Chinese are equally ignorant of geography and navigation; they have no methods for discovering the latitude and longitude of different places, and always, if possible, keep close to the shore. The vessels exhibited in the annexed plate are evidently ill adapted to a long voyage; nor is the three-masted junk, presented in the preceding plate, of a structure to contend with the tremendous gales so frequently experienced in the Chinese seas. The hull of these junks is of a curved form; the fore part, instead of being round, as is usual with European vessels, is square and flat like the stern, and both are elevated far above the deck; it is without a keel, and the diameter of the mainmast is sometimes equal to that of an English man of war, of sixty guns. The sails are wrought from the fibres of the bamboo, and are often furled and unfurled like a fan; the rudder is placed in an opening of the stern, and is usually taken up in sands and shallows. It frequently happens that one of these junks is the common concern of a hundred merchants, whose goods are lodged in separate compartments. A ship of the largest size carries one thousand tons and five hundred men, each of whom has his humble birth, containing a mat and a pillow. The compass is placed before an altar, on which burns a taper, composed of wax, tallow, and sandal wood dust, and divided into twelve equal divisions: which are intended to measure out the progress of the hours. Numbers of these vessels sail every season from Canton on commercial expeditions, and it is computed that ten thousand seamen perish annually in the Chinese seas. No one embarks in this perilous enterprize without taking a solemn farewel of his family and friends; and should it be his fate to return, his restoration is joyfully celebrated as a resurrection from death. It would, perhaps, be impossible to discover a man, who, like Sindbad, had made a seventh voyage. In one or two passages to Batavia the adventurer makes his fortune, the only object sufficiently stimulating to draw him from his native home.

NEAR WHAMPOA, CHINA.

Drawn & Engraved by Thos. & Willm. Daniell.

Published by Messrs. Longman, Hurst, Rees & Orme Paternoster Row, June 1.1810.

VIEW NEAR WHAMPOA.

FRENCH Island is opposite to Whampoa, whose stately pagoda forms a striking object in its sweet romantic scenery. Nothing indeed can exceed the beauty of the country in this vicinity. Vegetation is every where most luxuriant; and though subjected to the hand of art, the graces of nature are not obliterated, but combined with the comforts of convenience and the decorum of improved society. The river which retains the same commercial activity, here assumes a new character, for, dividing into many streams, at a little distance from its banks, it is traceable only by the sails of innumerable vessels that seem to glide in every direction through the fields, producing an appearance of some illusion of enchantment. Where every object, both on land and water, is strongly marked with novelty, the attention of the stranger is excited more and more in proportion as he advances into the country, and the effects of population multiply; and though he is often bewildered in the midst of so much variety, there is one little circumstance that seldom escapes his notice, evincing much dexterity in the Chinese boatmen: which is the frequent appearance of a man sitting alone in his vessel, steering it with one hand, holding the sail with the other, while with his foot he plies the oar; and in addition to which, so far is he from being embarrassed by these operations, he smokes his pipe with perfect tranquillity. The tree most conspicuous in the annexed plate is the palm or cajam tree, whose elegant foliage is employed in packing tea, in thatching houses, in fabricating water-proof garments, and various economical uses.

CHINESE TOMB.

Drawn & Engraved by Thoˢ. & Willᵐ. Daniell.

Published by Messʳˢ. Longman Hurst Rees & Orme Paternoster Row July 1, 1810.

CHINESE TOMB.

THE Chinese are remarkable for their tenderness to their dead, and evince the strongest attachment to the tombs of their ancestors. Custom, which reconciles them to the exposure of a helpless infant, revolts at the appearance of rudeness or neglect to an unconscious corpse. It is not uncommon for persons in affluence to procure magnificent coffins for their future remains: those appropriated to the higher classes are made of the most precious wood, pitched within, and varnished without, to prevent the emission of noxious effluvia. The body is carefully embalmed; and when finally removed to the family sepulchre, receives daily visits and prostrations from the affectionate relatives. The Chinese monuments are constructed of stone, and sometimes consist merely of a column either square, circular, or triangular, erected in a grove of cypress trees. The mausoleum exhibited in the plate is such as is proper only to families of distinction: it is detached from the mansion, and formed of three terraces, one over the other: on the uppermost of them is placed the door of the sepulchre. The same sentiment of reverence for the dead prevails in the lower orders: the poor man's coffin is made of coarse materials, and deposited in a little bed of earth, over which are planted dwarf trees, which it is the business of the survivors to keep clear of weeds. The sequestered spot is often visited with emotions of tenderness; and when no kinsman remains to trim the humble mound, its sanctity is still acknowledged and respected by the stranger, who may chance to direct his steps towards the nameless grave.

CHINESE GENTLEMAN.

Drawn & Engraved by Thos. & Willm. Daniell.

Published by Messrs. Longman, Hurst, Rees & Orme, Paternoster Row, July 1810.

CHINESE GENTLEMAN.

A CHINESE gentleman is here presented in his ordinary dress. He wears a jacket, and under it a loose vest descending to the ankles; his head is covered with a cap made of bamboo, and ornamented with red silk: the boots are large and of a peculiar shape; they are composed of satin; the soles of paper, very thick, made from the bamboo. In the right hand he holds a pipe, and suspends from one of his fingers a silk purse, containing the never-to-be-forgotten tobacco. This garden is like the former, embellished with an artificial rock, and relieved by trees of various foliage. On the terrace are ranged pots of the most rare and curious plants. Near the steps leading to an upper terrace is placed a seat made of porcelain. The building to the right is a part of the mansion; the small pagoda to the left is an ornamental object. The leisure of a Chinese gentleman is commonly devoted to smoking and chewing betel, to which is sometimes added the use of opium. The pleasures of society are here subordinate to the gratification of appetite: the table is loaded with delicacies, but elegant pleasures are wholly unknown. Literature is seldom cultivated for amusement, and authors are said to be more numerous than readers.

CHINESE LADY.

Drawn & Engraved by Thos. & Willm. Daniell.

Published by Messrs. Longman, Hurst, Rees & Orme, Paternoster Row, July 1, 1810.

CHINESE LADY.

ARTIFICIAL rocks are common in Chinese gardens, and when skilfully formed and judiciously introduced have a natural and picturesque effect; through these scenes water is often conducted with great taste, and their light bridges add both convenience and beauty. A lady of quality is here represented seated, with no better occupation than that of languidly moving her fan: her dress, though composed of richer materials, is not more elegant than that of her homely attendant: the hair is smoothed with oil, and confined in plaits to the crown of the head with a silver bodkin; on the forehead descends a peak of velvet, to which in full dress is added some ornament of diamonds or artificial flowers: she wears a vest of taffeta, and over it a loose robe with long sleeves. The changes and caprices of fashion are here unknown; the ladies live in seclusion, and when they go abroad are carefully concealed in their sedans. The wife never sits at the same table with her husband, and is rarely indulged with his society. The women are all reared in ignorance and imbecility; and women of rank have the additional misery of existing without even those feminine occupations which employ the lower orders. To a lady of quality it appears almost equally disgraceful to use her feet or her fingers: the common resource is smoking; and it is not unusual to see girls of nine or ten years of age furnished with a pipe, and wearing at their side a silk purse containing tobacco.

WHAMPOA PAGODA.

Drawn & Engraved by Thos. & Willm. Daniell.

Published by Messrs. Longman Hurst Rees & Orme Paternoster Row July 1810.

WHAMPOA PAGODA.

THE stately pagoda of Whampoa rises to an elevation of nearly 120 feet; and, like other edifices of the kind, is constructed of brick. From its summit there is a fine view of the adjacent mountains, and the extensive and varied navigation of the Canton river; from the declivity of the hill on which the pagoda stands to the edge of the water is a flourishing rice plantation: the vessel on the left with its single sail, is of the kind usually employed in conveying teas from the European factories at Canton to the East Indiamen stationed at Whampoa. When the wind proves unfavourable the sail is lowered, and the boat is navigated by ten or twelve men, who, by the help of bamboo poles, impel her through the water with considerable celerity. These vessels are obviously ill adapted to rough weather; but when a squall arises, the sailors discover admirable courage and dexterity: they have, in general, been trained to this occupation from early childhood, and are by law restricted from living on shore till they shall have acquired a sum sufficient to purchase a small demesne, including house and garden: a regulation that must certainly operate as a powerful incentive to industry, frugality, and perseverance.

SCENE ON THE CANTON RIVER.

Drawn & Engraved by Thos. & Willm. Daniell.

Published by [illegible] Longman, Hurst, Rees & Orme, Paternoster Row, July [illegible].

SCENE ON THE CANTON RIVER.

THIS view is selected from the Canton river, and exhibits the general aspect of that busy scene and various specimens of Chinese navigation. The greater part of these vessels are employed in trade, though many are kept for excursions of pleasure. The large vessel to the right is a passage boat: it is fitted up with much convenience and taste; and in these vessels the Europeans are accustomed to make their excursions on the Canton river. The minute distinctions of rank contribute materially to the variety and animation of the scene: the barge of a Mandarin and of every officer of state being known by appropriate insignia. Even at night it is customary to hang out lights, to designate the rank of those on board, which give a new interest to the watery spectacle; and the reflexions from these gaily painted lanterns trembling on the waves, the deep vibrations of the gong, and simple, but not ungrateful, melodies of the mariners, produce the most pleasing impressions on the mind of the European stranger.

HOE CHU FOU TOE A CHINESE FORT NEAR CANTON.

Drawn & Engraved by Thos. & Willm. Daniell.

Published by Messrs. Longman Hurst Rees & Orme, Paternoster Row, Augst. 1.1810.

HOE CHU FOU TOE, A CHINESE FORT NEAR CANTON.

THE exterior of this fortress conveys no idea of strength or extent: the walls are, however, mounted with several pieces of artillery; a large garrison, a governor's house, a temple, and several handsome edifices are enclosed within its battlements: the artillery is of little use. The Chinese, with their accustomed love of singularity, persist in preferring matchlocks to firelocks; their flint and steel are of the worst quality, and their gunpowder is execrable. Under such circumstances, it is not surprising they should prefer the musket to the sabre: but their favourite weapon is the bow, which the Tartars wield with peculiar ease and dexterity. There is, however, always something ludicrous in their military accoutrement: the arrow glances at the quilted petticoat; and the same hand furls the fan that brandishes the sabre.

SOUTH WEST VIEW OF CANTON.

Drawn & Engraved by Thos. & Willm. Daniell.

Published by Messrs. Longman, Hurst, Rees & Orme, Paternoster Row, Augt. 1 1810.

SOUTH-WEST VIEW OF CANTON.

THE vicinity of the mountains contributes materially to the salubrity of Canton, which, like Pekin, is several miles in circumference. It is the most considerable port in China, and almost the only place accessible to strangers. There is a large part even of Canton, called the Tartarean city, that no foreigner is permitted to enter: the streets, though narrow as alleys, are extremely straight, and flagged with round stones; the houses seldom exceed one story in height; the ground floor is laid out in a shop; and the loft above is merely a store; no accommodations are provided for the family, whose residence is always in another quarter. It is not usual to meet with either horses or carriages, but foot passengers are so numerous that it is not without difficulty even palanquins are carried through them. This sketch of Canton is taken from the south-west side of the river; the elegant row of buildings on the opposite bank consists of European factories, each distinguished by its national flag. The west fort, though destitute of strength, is a pleasing object. At night this scene appears to peculiar advantage: the water reflects a stream of light from the boats and houses, which are splendidly illuminated with lanterns. Fire works are often exhibited: a species of spectacle in which the Chinese eminently excel. In this animated scene it is pleasing to our countrymen to observe the superior elegance of the British factory; and so honourable is the character of the East India Company, that boxes of dollars bearing their stamp pass through China like bank notes in England. In such estimation is the commercial prosperity and probity of our country in that remote corner of the globe.

CHINESE BARBER.

Drawn & Engraved by Tho.s & Will.m Daniell.

Published by Mess.rs Longman, Hurst, Rees & Orme, Paternoster Row, Aug.t 1, 1810.

CHINESE BARBER.

IN China many trades and avocations are pursued in the open air. The barber carries about his moveable shop, and cheerfully traverses the streets, in search of employment. When he encounters a person willing to accept his services, he dexterously removes the bamboo pole, to which his load is attached from the shoulder, and begins the elaborate process. The utensil on his left hand, resembling a tripod, supplies the fire and water so essentially necessary to the tonsorial operations: the chest on his right hand contains the apparatus for shaving the head and beard, cleansing the ears, cutting the nails of the toes and fingers, and is easily converted into a seat for the welcome customer. The punctilious nicety of the Chinese on some occasions accords not with the general coarseness of their character, and their phlegmatic indifference to the decencies of life. With a singular degree of inconsistency, they attach great importance to the custom of cleansing the ears; but are very sparing of ablutions, and have even an habitual complacency for filth and vermin.

CHINESE LADY.

Drawn & Engraved by Thos. & Willm. Daniell.

Published by Messrs. Longman Hurst Rees & Orme, Paternoster Row.

CHINESE LADY.

IN this plate is represented a lady presiding in her garden retreat: she is precluded by her exalted rank from any occupation but smoking; and, except in holding her silk purse, or occasionally waving the fan, appears to have no use for her fingers. The dignity of her birth is sufficiently attested by the Lilliputian shoe. The practice of compressing the female foot is peculiar to the Chinese, and its origin has hitherto baffled all the efforts of industry and curiosity: it has been commonly attributed to jealousy; but that passion is at least equally powerful in Turkey and Hindostan, where it has produced no analogous absurdity. The liberty of the Chinese ladies in reality is not abridged by their lameness; they can saunter in the garden; they are permitted to go abroad in palanquins; and are in general even less restricted than other Asiatic females. It would, perhaps, be more reasonable to suppose that the compression of the female foot has originated in pride and arrogance than in cruelty and suspicion; and that it wants not defenders even in the sex who suffers as a badge of gentility, a constant line of demarcation between the noble and the vulgar. It is, however, remarkable that this custom has never been adopted by the Tartars, and, to whatever principle it may be referred, was unknown even in China in the tenth century.

CHINESE OF RANK.

Drawn & Engraved by Thos. & Willm. Daniell.

Published by Messrs. Longman Hurst Rees & Orme Paternoster Row Aug.t 1810.

A CHINESE OF RANK.

THIS plate presents an apartment in a Chinese mansion. The house, like all the habitations of the great, is surrounded with a high wall, over which the lofty trees of the garden are just visible; the floor is of stone, and corresponds with the columns supporting the edifice. In the compartments of the wall are hung frames of silk of various colours, with characters, which convey some moral axiom or religious precept. On the table are placed vases of porcelain, containing fruits and flowers: the lantern suspended near the window is used at night, when it is splendidly illuminated. The grave personage in the arm-chair is known by the beads on his neck to be a Mandarin of distinguished rank; and the badge worn on his breast, exhibiting the figure of a bird, intimates that he fills not a military but a civil department: the two attendants are ready to light his pipe, an operation frequently performed by a lens, or to replenish it with tobacco.

CHINESE JUNKS.

Drawn & Engraved by Tho.s & Will.m Daniell.

Published by Mess.rs Longman, Hurst, Rees & Orme, Paternoster Row Sept. 1810.

CHINESE JUNKS.

THE two foremost vessels lying at anchor are junks of four or five hundred tons burthen. The deformity of their structure on a near view, excites sensations of terror in the beholder. The bow, or fore-port, instead of being rounded after the European custom, is flat and square; a circular eye is painted on it, to intimate the necessity of vigilance and caution to the helmsman. Astern of them is a small trading vessel under sail. In the distance are other junks, those leviathans of the Chinese seas, whose perilous course cannot be contemplated by an European without emotions of pity and regret.

CHINESE PAVILLION.

Drawn & Engraved by Thos. & Willm. Daniell.

Published by Messrs. Longman Hurst Rees & Orme, Paternoster Row, Septr. 1, 1810.

CHINESE PAVILION.

THE principal object in the annexed plate is a Chinese pavilion, and may be considered as a fair specimen of this species of architecture. It is situated in a garden belonging to a mandarin of rank; the foundation is of stone, and the superstructure of wood; the pillars are all painted, varnished, and gilt, as are the roof and galleries. At some distance is a pagoda, probably erected to enrich the prospect from the pavilion. It is a common practice with the great, when they give entertainments, to receive their guests in a pavilion which generally opens on a green lawn, where singsongs or fireworks are exhibited for their amusement. In the imperial gardens each pavilion has a throne of state, which never fails to receive the obsequious homage of every passing visitor.

AN OFFERING TO THE GOD OF FIRE.

Drawn & Engraved by Thos. & Willm. Daniell.

Published by Messrs. Longman, Hurst, Rees & Orme, Paternoster Row, Septr. 1 1810.

AN OFFERING TO THE GOD OF FIRE.

THE subject of this plate represents a ceremony, common among the Chinese, which occurred some years since at Canton, when some junks having been accidentally burnt in the river, it was deemed expedient to offer a propitiatory sacrifice to the genius of fire. The scene is on the banks of the Tigris. On the shore is placed a large tray, in which are arranged the cups and saucers containing the sacred oblations: above it is suspended a large lanthorn, to which many smaller ones are attached; the smoke is produced by the combustion of paper: the persons bending before the tray, in an attitude of supplication, are merchants, solicitous to appease the vindictive deity: behind them is a group, composed of six priests clothed in red, attended by musicians, playing upon the patterra, and the gong, or loo. At the conclusion of the ceremony, the tea, rice, and sweetmeats, contained in the cups, are consumed. The Chinese have no religious assemblies, nor any stated seasons for public or private worship. They repair to the temples, which are always open, as often as they are prompted by hope or fear, to invoke the favour of their respective deities. To discover future events is the great incentive to this spurious devotion; and the mysteries of divination are not confined to the priesthood: each temple has its altar; on each altar is placed a wooden cup filled with sticks, on which are inscribed certain characters portentous of good or evil. To consult the oracle, nothing is necessary but to shake the cup till one of the sticks shall happen to fall; then referring to a book which is open for inspection, the enquirer, who can read, discovers some correspondent character, and annexed to it, some sentence declaring his happy or unhappy destiny.

VIEW IN A CHINESE GARDEN.

Drawn & Engraved by Thos. & Willm. Daniell.

Published by Messrs. Longman, Hurst, Rees & Orme, Paternoster Row, Sept. [illegible]

VIEW IN A CHINESE GARDEN.

IT is curious to remark, that in a country where good taste appears to be almost unknown, it should be so conspicuously displayed in the art of dressing the surface of the earth. It must nevertheless be acknowledged, that while in every other liberal or elegant art the taste of the Chinese is either puerile or barbarous in the extreme, in ornamental gardening they have shewn themselves capable of instructing nations greatly their superiors in every other species of intellectual culture. With them it would seem to be a general principle to suppress every sentiment, as well as to disguise every appearance, of nature; but in the arrangement and embellishment of grounds appropriated to elegant pleasures they take an opposite course, and wisely considering nature as their only true guide, aim only to follow her example, and to imitate or preserve her beauties; therefore, if we except their ridiculous attachment to artificial rocks, a Chinese garden presents few objects that good sense and good taste will not approve.

This plate gives only a glance into one of these luxurious scenes, where groves, and pavilions, and water are combined, not only to produce the charms of beauty and variety, but the comforts of coolness and shade.

A CHINESE MILITARY OFFICER.

Drawn & Engraved by Thos. & Wm. Daniell.

Published by Messrs. Longman Hurst Rees & Orme, Paternoster Row. Sept. 1. 1810.

A CHINESE MILITARY OFFICER.

THE conspicuous personage encumbered with military accoutrements is an officer of exalted rank. Over the usual dress is his uniform, consisting of an embroidered silk robe. In a case suspended to his side he carries the bow, which is made of wood, covered with horn; and on the other side his quiver with arrows. The flags on his shoulders are of silk, and their number announces the dignity of the wearer. From the crown of his helmet, which is of iron, issues a small spear, sheathed in a lock of dyed horse-hair. The same ornament is appended to the head of the pike, and is always deemed a mark of consideration: the bow-string is of silk: the arrows are pointed with steel. The scene of this view is a city gate, a station usually attended by a guard of soldiers.

CHINESE DUCK BOAT.

Drawn & Engraved by Tho.s & Will.m Daniell.

Published by Mess.rs Longman Hurst Rees & Orme Paternoster Row Oct.r 1. 1810.

A CHINESE DUCK BOAT.

THE scene is on the Tigris. A small village and a temple appear on the right. The near object is a duck boat, in which hundreds of those birds are reared for sale. This boat is only distinguished from others by the projections on each side, which are made light and strong with the bamboo, and intended to facilitate the egress of its amphibious crew. When the tide is low, it is secured by bamboos, and brought close to some mud bank or paddy ground, where the ducks are permitted to pick up worms for food. At the signal from their keeper, they begin to move with great order and decorum out of the boat; and when the signal is given for their return, they manifest their obedience by moving out of the water with the same promptitude and regularity. The structure of these vessels is extremely fragile; but the Chinese fishermen are too expert in swimming to incur much danger from the accidents common to their occupation. For children who are too young to have acquired the art, they use the precaution of fastening round the waist a dry gourd, which, should they happen to fall into the water, ensures them from drowning.

CAMOENS CAVE, MACAO.

Drawn & Engraved by Thos. & Willm. Daniell.

Published by Messrs. Longman, Hurst, Rees & Orme, Paternoster Row, Oct. [illegible]

CAMOENS' CAVE, MACAO.

IT is delightful to discover in a remote corner of Asia an object like Camoens' cave, consecrated to the memory of European genius. It is well known that the adventurous bard having too freely indulged his wit in satire, was disgraced by Francisco Barreto, the viceroy of Goa, and banished to Macao. Tradition still preserves some records of his residence. The stranger is still led to the top of the rock where he was accustomed to walk, and where the summer-house is now erected, commanding a view of the harbour of Macao: but it was in this romantic cave that he delighted to spend his leisure hours, forgetting past and present hardships in the luxurious exercise of his imagination. His exile was softened by the kindness he experienced; and he obtained a lucrative appointment, which enabled him in five years to realize a considerable fortune: but, like Spenser, he lost his all in shipwreck; and finally returned to Portugal as poor as he left it. He died at Lisbon in 1679, in his sixty-second year. The following lines, extracted from the seventh Lusiad, contain a brief but pathetic narrative of his life.

Ah! see how long, what perilous days, what woes,
On many a foreign coast around me rose,
As dragg'd by fortune's chariot wheels along,
I sooth'd my sorrows with the warlike song!
Wide ocean's horrors lengthening now around,
And now my footsteps trod the hostile ground;
Yet 'mid each danger of tumultuous war,
Your Lusian heroes ever claim'd my care;
As Canaa of old, ere self destroy'd,
One hand the pen, and one the sword employ'd.
Degraded now, by poverty abhorr'd,
The guest dependent at the lordling's board.
Now blest with all the wealth fond hope could crave,
Soon I beheld that wealth beneath the wave
For ever lost! myself escaped alone.
On the wild shore all friendless, hopeless, thrown,
My life, like Judah's, heaven-doom'd king of yore,
By miracle prolong'd. Yet not the more
To end my sorrows; woes succeeding woes,
Belied my earnest hopes of sweet repose.
In place of bays, around my brows to shed
Their sacred honours, o'er my destin'd head
Foul calumny proclaim'd the fraudful tale,
And left me mourning in a dreary jail.

COAST OF COCHIN CHINA.

Drawn & Engraved by Thos. & Willm. Daniell.

Published by Messrs. Longman, Hurst, Rees & Orme Paternoster Row Octr. 1810.

COAST OF COCHIN CHINA.

THE land in this view, generally seen by navigators in their passage from China to Bengal, is the mountainous region of Cochin China. It is a bold but barren coast, and bears few traces of vegetation, with none of culture. No high forest trees are seen sheltering the rocky summits, which the approaching tempest often overshadows with dark recumbent clouds. No rice plantations are discovered on the shore. The land, like the ocean, wears a rude but sublime aspect of desolation.

PEDRO BRANCO, STRAITS OF MALACCA.

Drawn & Engraved by Thos. & Willm. Daniell.

Published by Messrs. Longman Hurst Rees & Orme Paternoster Row [illegible]

PEDRO BRANCO.

PEDRO Branco, which has been thought to resemble the Bass rock in the Frith of Forth, is situated at the entrance of the Straits of Malacca, where it stands like a lonely watch-tower in the ocean. It is descried from a considerable distance, being easily distinguished by the tremendous breakers ever dashing against its base. So violent is the surge at this point, that the boldest navigator might rejoice to leave it behind him: yet, even in tempestuous weather, Malay proas are often seen near it. Pedro Branco derives its name from its white surface; it is seldom ascended by human feet, and the only strangers to whom its hospitality is not suspicious are flocks of aquatic birds, who commonly visit it to snatch an interval of repose from the fatigues of their aerial voyage.

CAPE RICARDO, STRAITS OF MALACCA.

Drawn & Engraved by Thoˢ & Willᵐ Daniell.

Published by Messʳˢ Longman Hurst Rees & Orme Paternoster Row Octʳ 1. 1810.

CAPE RICHARDO.

ON approaching Cape Richardo, the voyager again recognizes canoes, proas, and Malays. He again beholds, with a mixture of admiration and regret, a luxurious yet indigent country, favoured by nature, but neglected by man, producing every thing but the arts of life; the knowledge, taste, and civilization, which can flourish only with an enlightened people. Cape Richardo, the most conspicuous object in the plate, is a scene of perpetual beauty and fertility, where the energy of vegetation is never exhausted, and luxury is spontaneously offered by nature. In the profusion of delicious fruits native to the soil, the mangosteen deserves to be mentioned, as perhaps the most exquisite. To the east of the Cape appears the main land of Malacca, the tops of whose distant mountains are enveloped in clouds, which during the rainy season pour down continual torrents. The country presents only the rude dwellings of its aboriginal inhabitants. The passage of the Straits of Malacca is commonly difficult, if not perilous: tremendous storms are frequent; and the water-spout, one of the most sublime objects on the ocean, may sometimes inspire fear even in the experienced mariner.

While from the left approaching, we descry
A liquid column tow'ring shoot on high;
Its foaming base an angry billow sweeps,
Where curling billows rouse the fearful deeps;
While round and round the fluid vortex flies,
Scattering drear night and horror through the skies.

FALCONER.

FOWL ISLAND, BAY OF BENGAL.

Drawn & Engraved by Thos. & Willm. Daniell.

Published by Messrs. Longman, Hurst, Rees & Orme, Paternoster Row, Nov. 1, 1810.

FOWL ISLAND, BAY OF BENGAL.

FOWL Island, though seldom explored by voyagers but for the purpose of procuring fresh water, is often visited by fleets of canoes from Ava, immense shoals of fish being discovered in the vicinity of its coast. Having completed their freight, the mariners spread their fish to dry on the beach, and afterwards pack it carefully for their home-bound voyage. These industrious fishermen are observed to bear a close resemblance to the Malays; and, like them, are active, expert, and enterprising. They wear a singular ornament, in shape not unlike a speaking trumpet; it is made either of bamboo wood, turtle shells, or silver, which is inserted in the ear, but for what purpose it is difficult to conceive. Ava, which appears in the distance, is a fertile and highly cultivated country; and has lately attracted the notice of Europe by the appellation of the Bisman empire. From the interesting account of major Symes's embassy, it appears to have made considerable advances in knowledge and civilization. Polygamy is not authorized; and women, though treated with little tenderness or respect, are not doomed to servitude and captivity. The popular religion is that of Boodh, a faith which preceded the doctrines of Brama in Hindostan, and still retains many followers in China. The religion and laws of Ava, though immediately derived from the neighbouring kingdom of Arracan, are traced with great probability to Ceylon. The Birmans are, however, happily exempted from the restrictions of cast established in that island; and disclaim many other superstitious prejudices, which both with the Hindoos and the Chinese retard the progress of improvement. They are active and intrepid, and possess habits of ebriety and diligence: their civil code is in general dictated by justice and humanity: and the poorest individual is instructed to read and write in the vulgar tongue.

NEAR GANGWAUGH COLLY, ON THE RIVER HOOGLY.

Drawn & Engraved by Thos. & Willm. Daniell.

Published by Messrs. Longman, Hurst, Rees & Orme Paternoster Row Novr. 1810.

NEAR GANGWAUCOLLY, ON THE HOOGLY.

THIS view is bounded by impenetrable forests; trees of gigantic growth rise among the underwood which overhangs the banks of the Hoogly, and forms a safe covert for the most fierce and formidable animals. The wild hog and buffalo are natives of this jungle; venomous snakes are nurtured in its luxurious verdure; and tygers, issuing from these delicious shades, are often bold enough to leap on the boats that ply near the coast: yet the deer, and other animals of the gentlest nature, are still found in the vicinity of their ferocious foes. The Hoogly is the western branch of the Ganges, and held so sacred by the Gentoos that they even consider it an enviable privilege to expire in its waves. This persuasion sufficiently explains their intrepidity in bathing in a river where alligators are constantly lurking for the unwary victim. To an European it is difficult to conceive that such an Eden should be tenanted by creatures so destructive. The cocoa, the most graceful of the palm tribe, is here familiar to the eye; and that most singular and picturesque of all vegetable productions, the banian, appears in full beauty. It is this fig-tree, that, to use the language of Milton,

> Spreads her arms
> Branching so broad and long, that in the ground
> The bended twigs take root. And daughters grow
> About the mother tree, a pillar'd shade
> High overarched, and echoing walks between.

The banian puts forth shoots, which having reached a certain length, strike into the ground, and produce a rapid succession of younger trees, destined in their turn to become the parent stocks of a numerous progeny. The banian is a symbol of pastoral peace and patriarchal longevity: it is the asylum of animals totally dissimilar in habits and dispositions, who subsist on its fruits, and are protected by its foliage. The peacock here unfolds his splendid plumage; doves nestle on the topmost boughs, and tribes of monkeys leap and chatter among the branches. Beneath its shade, the herdsman watches his flock; the manufacturer plies at the loom; the musician touches his pipe; whilst the Bramin, abstracted from all sublunary objects, performs his solitary though not silent devotions.

NEAR CUCRAHATTEE, ON THE RIVER HOOGLY.

Drawn & Engraved by Tho.s & Will.m Daniell.

Published by Mess.rs Longman, Rees, Orme & Co. Paternoster Row Nov.r 1.1830.

NEAR CUCRAHAUTTEE, ON THE RIVER HOOGLY.

THIS view is taken from a spot near the Hoogly, embellished by nature with all the exuberance of vegetation peculiar to Bengal. The level face of the country is a defect abundantly compensated by the variety and magnificence of the foliage; but the eye is perpetually offended by pieces of stagnant water, which generate impure air and myriads of insects, incessant in their persecution of the human species. Of these the most formidable are the musquitoes, which are merely gnats of a gigantic size. It is curious to observe how completely sensation is subdued by custom and the operation of superstitious prejudice. The poor Hindoo, anxious to ensure his performance of those daily ablutions which constitute an essential part of worship, erects his hut on the margin of these polluted streams, and felicitates himself on the circumstance that exposes him to probable danger and inevitable inconvenience.

VIEW OF CALCUTTA FROM THE GARDEN REACH.

Drawn & Engraved by Thos. & Willm. Daniell.

Published by Messrs. Longman, Hurst, Rees & Orme Paternoster Row Novr. 1.1810.

VIEW OF CALCUTTA FROM THE GARDEN REACH.

CALCUTTA is situated on that part of Bengal called the Sunderbund, a woody peninsula, which from its triangular figure has acquired the appellation of the Delta of the Ganges. It is the Hoogly, the western branch of that magnificent river, which is here visible. A few miles below the town, the stream becomes narrower, and at Garden Reach is but twice the breadth of the Thames at London. It is from a situation near this part the present view of Calcutta is taken. On the south side of the river is erected Fort William, part of which appears in the plate. Between the fort and the town is a broad walk called the Esplanade, and frequented by people of all descriptions for air and amusement. Contiguous to the Esplanade is the government house, a superb edifice, approached by four colossal gates emblazoned with the Britannic arms. To the west of this palace appears the council house; and almost in the same line the new church. The buildings are covered with chunaur, a species of stucco possessing the delicacy and lustre of marble. The houses at Calcutta are without chimneys, and have universally terrace roofs: those on the Esplanade are insulated from each other, and approached by a flight of steps under a projecting portico; each is surrounded by a magnificent colonnade, and has the air of a palace. The streets are spacious, and from the diversity of European and oriental manners, present a scene of inexhaustible variety and amusement. The chariot often comes in contact with the palankeen; and the phaeton is seen lightly rolling before the litter-like hackney, a covered cart slowly drawn by bullocks, and appropriated to the service of secluded females. Amidst the promiscuous concourse of people and equipages stalks a tall meagre crane, nicknamed the adjutant, which performs the useful office of scavenger, and is perfectly familiar with the inhabitants. This bird is remarkable for the slowness of its movements, and often stands on some roof, dropping its head with ludicrous solemnity, and looking as abstracted as a fakir at his devotions. The river presents a scene of almost equal animation and variety.

OLD FORT GAUT, CALCUTTA.

Drawn & Engraved by Thos. & Willm. Daniell.

Published by Messrs. Longman, Hurst, Rees & Orme Paternoster Row Novr. 1 1810.

OLD FORT GAUT, CALCUTTA.

WITHIN the walls of this fort is the black hole, whose name is eternized by the sufferings of Mr. Holwell and his ill-fated companions in 1756. The low range of buildings attached to the fort consists of warehouses belonging to the East India Company. The Gaut, or flight of steps leading from the river, is usually the landing place, where strangers are immediately surrounded by palankeens, and a train of natives, importuning them to accept their respective services. Near this spot it is a daily practice with men, women, and children, to bathe promiscuously in the river; and Bramins are here often seen performing their devotions. Calcutta rose about 120 years ago on the scite of Cossimpoor, an inconsiderable Indian village, and was originally included in the small number of edifices adjoining the fort: but the splendor of the British arms produced a sudden change in its aspect: the bamboo roof suddenly vanished; the marble column took place of brick walls; princely mansions were erected by private individuals; hospitals were endowed with royal munificence, and colleges with republican liberality. Calcutta is now the metropolis of British India, the seat of a powerful and prosperous empire, which has already communicated to those remote regions a portion of its national laws and liberties; and is probably destined to disseminate those arts and sciences which have conferred such honourable distinction on the people of Europe.